The 20 Week Life Overhaul Challenge

Organize Your Life In 20 Weeks To Set You On The Path To Happiness And Realizing Your Potential

Table of Contents

Introduction

This book contains proven steps and strategies on how to commit yourself to your personal improvement by creating healthy habits, gaining a better perspective in life, and having a healthier mindset.

Picking up this book is guaranteed to change your life, as it serves as your ultimate step-by-step guide to personal success. Get ready to improve relationships, have a youthful body, gain charisma and self-confidence, lose your debts, permanently fix your finances, and more as you progress with your personal challenges. At the same time, this book comes with troubleshooting techniques to help you get rid of anything that stops you from improving yourself. The best part is that this challenge can help you improve all facets of your life.

If you are ready to learn to love yourself and become a better worker, companion, and family member, then this is the book for you. Learn all the secrets to becoming the best possible version of you. At the end of this book, you will unleash the power that you have to change your life for the better. The best part is that all improvements you make can be permanent. All you need to do is to commit to change.

Setting the Course

When you picked up this book, you already knew there was something wrong with the way you handle life. What you want is a reboot, a way to get back to square one. However, you might be wondering how this is possible. Before you start to feel regret, you should be aware that there is still hope for you.

What You Need is an overhaul.

When you dread Mondays because you have to get out of bed to face your responsibilities, you already know you need a major life change. You may be thinking that life is not fair, and it is definitely not right that you see your neighbor having the time of his life, eating his breakfast and reading the paper when you barely have time to prepare for work. However, why are you having difficulty with time and energy and your neighbor is not? What are you doing wrong?

Now, why do you need an overhaul? You need it badly in order to design life patterns and processes that work out for you. At the same time, this fix also allows you to realize what you are doing wrong.

Making Your Own Prescription

When you need to rethink your life and live it using another approach, it does not mean you have to do what your neighbor does. You need to take your own steps toward improvement, and create a recipe of actions that work best with your life goals and skills.

Speaking of plans, what you are about to do for the next 20 weeks is to identify your problems and what causes them. After that, you are going to come up with your personal solution. Take note that nobody can teach you what to do – this book only serves as your guide on how to create your own action plan. There are many suggestions here, of course.

Start on a Monday

Why choose the worst day of the week? That is because Monday is normally the day when people set the pace they are going to keep for the rest of the week. If you are wondering why you hate Mondays, it is because that day reminds you of all the responsibilities you have as an adult. It is also the day that you reconnect with the rest of the world. For these reasons, it is only appropriate that you also start changing your relationship with Mondays.

Starting today, think of Monday as the day of promise. That means you are going to resolve to make a major life change at the start of the week. The good thing about that you are also resolving to make every Monday special and exciting.

Your Goals

What you need to achieve every week is a major life change, which means you will fix one facet of your life every seven days. Seven days should be enough for you to troubleshoot one aspect and think of a solution. At the same time, you have to make a commitment to practice that solution throughout the program. You need to promise yourself not to fall back into old bad habits once you find a remedy.

Results

By the end of this 20-week challenge, you will enjoy the following benefits:

1. More control over your life

2. Good health

3. A clean home that calms and rejuvenates you

4. A happier perspective in life

5. Improved relationships

6. Resolved financial problems

7. More energy to face your tasks

8. More free time to spend

9. Great organizational skills

10. More focus on your personal goals

Should you resolve to keep these goals in mind and become ready to change your life for the better, then you are ready to start your first week. The next chapter will show you how.

Week 1: Change Your Perspective

Since you are going to start your commitment on a Monday, it is about time to have a talk with yourself. What is wrong with the first day of the workweek? Is it because of the traffic or the fact that you have to wake up early again?

At this point, you already know there is no stopping Mondays. They are going to come every week. However, a Monday is not that different from a Tuesday. The rest of the weekdays involve virtually the same routine as a Monday, but you have to understand that Mondays require special treatment as the start of the workweek. It is probably because you hate having to go to work and everything involved with that.

It's How You See Things

If there is a best first step to take when it comes to overhauling your life, it is changing your perspective. The way you view your activities allows you to focus or not focus your energy on them. If you do not deem an activity important, there is a big chance you will think it is okay to delay or neglect it.

There are several ways to improve your perspective. The best way, however, is to eliminate the following habits:

1. Expecting the worst

If you always imagine the worst case, then you will have a hard time enjoying any day of the week. Try optimism instead, and you might realize that you have much to look forward to.

2. Dreading

You may dread Sundays because right after Sunday comes Monday. Nevertheless, why would you feel like that? Instead of dreading the start of the week, think of it as an opportunity to start fresh and improve. Remember that you have weekends for rest, so starting the week should not be a problem.

Dreading is a bad habit because it sets the expectation that you are going to have a bad experience. However, instead of predicting the bad, it will do you good to look forward to the good things. If you go to work on Mondays, then it is a good thing. That means you will receive a paycheck.

3. Putting focus on things you are not currently facing

If you are putting too much energy on your ex or where you are going this weekend, you may be neglecting to prioritize the present. Before you know it, the day has already ended, and you did not complete all the tasks you needed to accomplish.

When changing your perspective, make it a point to include the time on it, so instead of focusing on the past or the future, pay attention to what is in front of you. That enables you to see your current situation better and address it promptly.

4. All-or-nothing thinking

Always remember that no one is forcing you to do anything in this world, so there is no such thing as all-or-nothing. Stop thinking that everything you do should be done otherwise you face serious consequences, like something bad will happen to you and your family. The better way to look at things you need to do is that they are your choice.

5. Reluctance to let go

You need to understand that bad things happen, and most of the time, there is no use beating yourself up over these occurrences. Starting today, learn to let go of the things you cannot control. You can then realize can cope with your day much more easily.

Resolve to be Happy

Why do you want to change your perspective and why should you start your life's overhaul with this task? The reason is simple: you will want to live your life to the fullest if you have a mission to be happy. Do not aim just to have it – make it your obligation to yourself.

For seven days, list all the things that make you happy within the week. It could be as simple as being able to have coffee by yourself in your favorite diner or being able to sleep for eight hours. This will be a list of everything you are thankful for. Make a journal out of this, and resolve to write it before you go to bed.

You will find that after writing down all the things that make you happy during the day that you are looking forward to the next day. You will feel that, just like today, tomorrow will also be full of surprises.

Week 2: Improve your Home

Now that you are on the second week of this challenge, it is time to focus on your home and your work area. For this week, you are going to resolve to remove all the items you do not need, and make your home a place you can rejuvenate your mind and body.

If you are too tired to get out of bed in the morning, and you do not even want to go home at the end of the day, then you need to assess the way your house makes you feel. If your home does not make you feel relaxed, then you need to put some work into it. Here are some tips on how to improve your home's ambience.

1. Clean your house.

One of the reasons you find your home wearisome is because it is not clean. Starting today, find time every day to tidy up your home and assign a day for general cleaning.

2. Spend time at home.

Do not be a stranger to your own house – remember you purchased this home for a reason. For that reason, see to it that you spend time at home as much as possible.

3. Make use of natural light.

Sunlight is good for setting a good mood. Raise the blinds and part the curtains in the morning. If you think the sunlight is too harsh, you can put white rice paper on your windows to dampen it.

4. De-clutter your home.

Make sure you throw away everything you are not using anymore. Free up space and make sure that all clutter disappears. The moment you free up space, you will be inspired to buy furniture and decors that works best with your current lifestyle.

5. Do not bring your work home.

Make your home your sanctuary. For that reason, make sure you separate it from your office. If you are telecommuting, see to it that you work in an area that is separate from the space where you relax.

6. Have a favorite chair or spot.

You will have better ownership of your home if you see to it that you have a spot you love. Buy the furniture you like to use and use it frequently. That way you can always come home to relax in your favorite spot.

Week 3: Resolve to Get Rid of Your Debts

This week, you are going to get rid of one reason that you never have peace of mind. Starting today you are going to make a solid financial plan to ensure you eliminate all your debts and prevent more debt in the future.

Make a List of All the Things You Need to Pay

If you are making a living, knowing everything about your financial resources is a must. See to it that you know if you make enough money by listing of all your expenditures. If possible, prepare an annual and a monthly list of expenses.

As a rule, you want to make sure you can pay for your bills and grocery shop before you reward yourself or make other unnecessary investments. If your list shows you have too little money for what you spend, you have two options: drop some expenses you can live without or find another source of income.

Account for All Your Invisible Expenses

If you have been wondering where all your money goes and you always come up short when it comes to paying your bills, you need to check on your invisible expenses. These expenses are normally not accounted for in your financial lists, but they are always there. They are normally those tiny expenditures you make every day, such as buying snacks from the vending machine or getting a pack of cigarettes. When they accumulate, you will certainly notice that these purchases are more than just loose change.

If you normally wonder why you do not have money in your wallet at the end of the day, these invisible expenses are usually the culprit. Make sure you minimize or do without them.

Make Sure You are Settling Your Debts

Most people feel they are wading in a pool of debt, but it will be easier to settle them if a payment plan is created.

Week 4: Have a Good Relationship with Your Job

Now that you are almost halfway done with this challenge, you should start to learn how to enjoy the way you spend your days. Yes, this means you have to come to terms with your relationship with your work and the work environment.

Do You Love Your Job?

Be honest with yourself – what are the reasons you are holding on to your job? To evaluate that, answer the following questions truthfully:

1. Do you feel that the work you do brings you personal advancement?

2. Do you like the challenge it brings you, and do you feel valuable at work?

3. Do you like your company culture and goals?

4. Do you think you are compensated fairly?

If you say yes to most of these questions, then it is very likely that you actually enjoy what you do. If not, make a plan on how to improve your situation.

Get on the Same Page with the Management

If you are having problems at work and you think the management can address them, then take this week to talk to your immediate supervisor to work together to improve your situation.

If you feel you are taking on too many tasks in a day and you are losing your drive, maybe you can arrange with your supervisor to delegate some tasks to your colleagues. At the same time, if you feel it is impossible to beat your deadlines, it might be possible for your supervisor to give an extension.

If You Feel You Need a Major Change

Perhaps you have been thinking about pursuing another career, and you might want to consider that thought. It is very possible that you dislike your work environment because you truly want to do something else.

Consider another career landscape if you truly feel you will grow better in another field. This way, you have the opportunity to hone your other skills and pursue your passions.

Week 5: Get a Hobby

Do you often feel burnt out? You may not be spending enough time for yourself. This week, resolve to keep a hobby, and make sure you include it in your schedule.

Pay Attention to Your Interests

People who tend to spend too much time on work sometimes forget that they have interests. When you feel you have outgrown your hobbies you used to enjoy, you might be missing something from your life. You might even feel you have not had fun for a long time.

If you feel like you have forgotten what it is like to have a hobby, take the weekend off and look at pictures that show you doing an activity of interest. Remember how you used to enjoy it, and think about the reasons you stopped doing it. If you feel you only stopped that hobby because you became too busy working or juggling responsibilities at home, then you simply are having a time-management problem. That, of course, can be easily resolved by allotting a day for your hobby in your monthly or weekly schedule.

Enroll in a Class or Do it With Your Friends

To ensure you have time for your hobbies, sign up for a club or a class, or enjoy the hobby with your friends. This requires you to attend scheduled meetings and see to it that you are honing your skills in the process. At the same time, you can easily block a date in your calendar for these activities.

Bring Your Hobby to Work

If you find it impossible to squeeze your hobby time into your busy schedule, you can opt to bring your hobby to work instead. Spend your break time to learn a new song or assemble a toy. You will feel that you spent your break more productively when you do this.

Read About Your Interests

If you are spending most of your idle time online, use that free time to look for anything related to your hobbies and interests. Window shop online or find people with similar interests that have made a living out of their hobbies. That may motivate you to hone your skills in your passion and give you more reason to pursue it.

Week 6: Use Your Breaks

If you feel you cannot last an entire shift at work, then you may not be taking enough breaks. This week, make sure you understand the value of your allotted time off and use it to make yourself more efficient.

That 15-minute Break is Important

Getting your mind off work and doing something else for 15 minutes allows you to reenergize your brain and refocus. If you believe you have been stuck at the beginning of your task and you are at a loss over how to finish it, take a break. That provides you some breathing room to clear your mind and become mindful of the activity you are supposed to do.

Maximize Your Lunch Break

Your lunch break is very important because you can use it to buy yourself some extra time. If you cannot afford to eat breakfast and exercise before going to work, 45 minutes worth of time off can buy you time to grab brunch, hit the gym, shower, and then go back to the office.

Lunch breaks are also excellent for taking naps, especially if you just got out of a grueling 90-minute meeting. After 20 to 30 minutes of napping, you will feel more refreshed, making you more productive and creative.

Get Up from the Chair

See to it that you turn off the monitor and leave your cubicle during breaks. Doing so allows your mind and body to get rid of work-related stress, thanks to a quick change of environment. Go for a walk in a nearby park and do some deep breathing exercises or meditation.

With these points in mind, ensure you forget the idea that taking fewer breaks means that you are working harder. Most of the time, those who do not take breaks often space out during tasks or find themselves wasting time on social media. With your mind and body constantly refreshed every two hours, you will find that you do not need to work overtime. At the same time, taking your time off also allows you to see your workplace as a positive environment by warding off work-related stress.

Week 7: Get Out of Town

This week, resolve to try out new places. Plan an out of town trip this coming weekend, and if possible, make it an extended vacation by cashing out some of your vacation days.

Why Vacation Leaves are Important

Vacations are important for everyone because they improve your productivity and creativity when you get back to work. If you feel you have been slacking off at work lately because you feel work-related stress or you are totally burned out, taking a vacation may provide you with the motivation you need to revitalize your performance. At the same time, it is helpful to know that people who take vacations live 20 percent longer than those who slave away nonstop at their desks.

Vacations are also great for rekindling your relationship with your family and friends, and they can serve as valuable time to spend with yourself. Not only will you feel rested, but you can also find the inspiration you need to get your creativity back.

If you are worried about the money you are going to lose when you take vacations, do not fret – you are definitely going to gain more when you take an adventure outside the office once in a while. With added productivity and creativity, plus a healthier mindset and body, you no longer need to use sick leaves as often. With a body and mind prepared for better performance, you might even qualify for a promotion soon.

Tips When Taking Your Vacation

1. Do not check your email or answer work-related phone calls.

Only answer your phone if it is a real emergency. You are on vacation to escape work, not to stay involved in it.

2. Delegate tasks while you are away.

If you tend to worry about your responsibilities when you are away for a couple of days, assign them to someone you trust and who is capable of handling them. Not only does delegating get the work done more efficiently, upper management may also take notice of your impressive leadership skills.

3. Take every opportunity to take your leaves.

Do not stop at just planning for this weekend – plan your vacation for the rest of the year. Do not think about the cash conversion and take a trip instead. You are doing your company more good by taking vacations since you get better work ideas while you are away.

The perks do not end there. By booking your vacations in advance, you can also save on travel tickets and hotels as well.

Week 8: Do Something Out of the Box

Most people feel burned out when they do not feel reasonably challenged. If you think that excitement has left your life, kill that boredom and do something out of the ordinary this week.

Creativity is Necessary

If you tend to do the same thing over and over again and continually reap rewards for doing so, you are bound to feel boredom. Boredom is good because it signals you to get on with your life and look for advancement.

You are definitely craving for a change when you wake up feeling bored. The best way to deal with that is to change your approach in all your tasks and create a new, unique schedule or activity.

Brainstorm

If you want to think outside the box, list all the possible approaches to a task you can do. Doing so also helps you become aware of all your other skills and of ways to test them. This becomes a perfect opportunity to receive feedback about your other skills.

Let your creative juices flow freely, so you can think up unorthodox solutions. Remember that brainstorming is not actually about finding out what works but imagining all the possible approaches to a specific situation. Once you finished listing all possible methods, you can narrow down to a specific approach.

If you need to deliver a report at work, and you know you are great at creating music, then you should compose a musical score for your PowerPoint presentation to make it more engaging. Not only does that help you drive the point more by setting the mood for your audience, you also develop your composition skills, as well.

Look at Situations Differently

Turn anything you need to do upside down and examine it from another angle. You may find there are many other methods when you look at situations from a different perspective. For example, if you are writing a report about how to improve sales, assume the position of your consumers instead of looking at your marketing strategies from your company's perspective.

Try Something New

Aside from taking on a different perspective, make it a point to do something new this week. It does not have to be something outrageous – just make sure you do something that enhances your day. Try a new dish or drink tea instead of coffee. Do anything that is not part of your usual routine.

This way, you can train yourself to be comfortable even outside of your comfort zone. When you do this more often, you will feel less anxious when you encounter new experiences, and you may even begin to embrace them.

Week 9: Improve Time Management

If you feel you are having a hard time completing all of your commitments starting from Week 1, think about this: you can do all the things you want to do if you know how to manage your time. This week, minimize or get rid of that challenge by following these tips:

1. Carry a planner and list your schedule. Not only does a planner help you keep track of blocked-off dates and times, but it also helps you monitor your progress with all the tasks listed there.

2. Make sure you list all the activities you think are important in your planner, with a specific to-do time and date. That means you are also keeping an appointment with yourself.

3. Place a Do Not Disturb sign on the door or on top of your desk. That should serve as a signal to everyone around you that you are trying to get things done, and you do not want to be disturbed.

4. Just because your phone rang or an email notification popped up, that does not mean you have to attend to it right away. Make people aware that you attend to these tasks at a specific schedule. Make other people stick to your best-to-reach times.

5. Schedule all your time off and any forms of interruption. While you need to pull yourself away from your tasks from time to time, make sure these times are specifically tied to a schedule. That way, you can manage your time better.

6. Do not spend overtime at work unless your job depends on it. Remember that you are only required to work within your shift.

7. If there is something that can be done within two minutes, do it immediately. That means you need to return every item you picked up back to its proper place and put your dirty clothes in the hamper right away.

8. Spend five minutes to think about what you want to achieve before starting any task. With a goal in mind, you are teaching yourself to find the most efficient steps to accomplish a task. Also, stop being indecisive. Think of a great plan right away, and stick to the beautiful finished product in your head.

With these tips in mind, you may find that you can fit most of your activities into the day.

Week 10: Assert Yourself

If you wonder how people view you in any relationship you are in and you tend to feel undervalued, then you may need to take a better look at where you stand in your relationships. If you tend to feel alone and left to your own devices most of the time, you need to start advocating for yourself. That will be your focus this week.

Let Other People Know How You Feel

Being assertive takes time, and this week is a good time to start practicing. Why do you need to assert your needs instead of waiting for others to be sensitive to them? The reason is simple – other people cannot guess what is on your mind.

Being able to tell other people what is on your mind helps you create harmonious relationships and ensures that you eliminate toxic relationships. Being assertive allows you and other people to enter into a compromise where both parties win, so instead of guessing what people are thinking about, you have the opportunity to enter a healthy discussion and offer a mutually beneficial resolution.

Tips on How to Express Yourself Better

1. Practice saying no.

Rejecting offers and requests from time to time is anything but selfish. Being able to say no allows you to build boundaries and express your belief that you have the right to draw a line. This way, you never have to spread yourself too thin or trouble yourself with things and circumstances you cannot control.

2. Avoid feelings of guilt.

Being assertive is difficult, especially if you have been passive most of your life. However, you have to accept that it is impossible to please everybody. Let go of guilt and accept the truth: there is nothing wrong with saying what you truly feel. For that reason, you should not feel like a bad person when you state what is on your mind.

3. Be direct and calm.

When speaking your mind, get straight to the point. Do not express yourself in a passive-aggressive way, and avoid playing mind games. At the same time, say what you feel about a pressing issue – do not attack the person with generalizations about his entire personality.

4. Listen and offer a compromise.

When you tell others what you think, make sure you also validate their thoughts about the issue at hand. Remember that assertiveness means you are willing to lay your cards on the table and hear the other side, as well. If you feel the other party has an opposing opinion, offer a compromise or a mutually beneficial solution.

Week 11: Find Your Motivation

Everyone falls into a slump. Even motivational speakers experience times when they feel down. When you feel that most of the time, you do not know how to channel positive thinking to get yourself into a lighter mood. This week will allow you to learn techniques on how to find motivation, even during days that seem dark.

Think About That Big Goal

When you feel you are sinking into your problems or you simply lack the will to get out of the house and face the day, take the time to think about your biggest goal that you need to achieve while you still have the energy and youth to reach it.

Many people feel they should just give up on everything because they have too many things to accomplish. When you feel bombarded by different aspects of your life, focus on a single goal. What is that single accomplishment you need to make in order to feel you have lived your life to the fullest? When you focus on that goal, you will realize that you have been fixating on too many minor issues. Take your mind away from these issues, and remind yourself that your mission is to achieve that single goal that defines your dreams.

Make Your Commitment Public

If you want to push yourself, make sure every support system you have is aware of what you want to pursue. Post your commitments on your Facebook wall, or gather everyone over dinner to say that you are going to quit smoking or you are going for that promotion. Trust that people will want to see you succeed and that they will contribute to your progress.

Place Goals Where You Can See Them

Write your goals and put them on the refrigerator door. If you want to remind yourself of what you want to achieve every time you wake up, put it on the ceiling above your bed. This can put you in the right mind frame from the very start of the day.

Week 12: Focus on Improving Your Health

Something that has been circulating for a while in social media is that your body is not a temple but a forest. That means you are capable of nourishing your body and making it capable of handling your needs again.

It is never too late to pay attention to your health, and by focusing on improving your physical and mental condition, you will soon be able to perform at the top of your game. At the same time, having a healthy diet and committing to exercise does not mean you have to limit yourself. Here are some tips to help you get started on living a healthy lifestyle without having to commit to strict regimens.

1. Eat breakfast.

Breakfast truly is the most important meal of the day because it allows you to energize yourself to make it through the day. Even if you are not hungry, make it a point to eat something before you head out to work or school.

2. Stretch once in a while.

Your muscles are elastic and whenever you stretch them, they become more nimble. Stretching also improves blood flow. If your lifestyle involves a lot of sitting, stand up once in a while and do an overhead stretch with your arms. Also, make it a point to spend at least two minutes stretching after you get out of bed.

2. Enjoy the sunlight.

Besides its essential healing properties, sunlight is also the best source of Vitamin D. If you take a weekend out of town, spend some time on the trail. If you are just staying home, spend some time in the backyard.

3. Avoid fast food as much as you can.

It might be a pain to prepare whole foods, but still make it a point to enjoy home-cooked meals. If you cannot cook your own meals, eat meals in a restaurant where whole foods are on the menu. Remember that fast food provides poor sources of energy and contribute to health issues like obesity.

4. Change your diet.

Make it a point to eventually substitute all the unhealthy foods you eat with something that gives you proper nourishment. You do not have to start big right away – begin eating healthy by substituting that donut with bananas and fresh blueberries. Try coffee with just two sugars and a single cream.

5. Do not eat until you feel stuffed.

You should eat to stop feeling hunger, and if you make it a point to eat until you are too full, then you are doing it wrong. Try decreasing your portions.

6. Have mini-workouts.

If you cannot visit the gym, then treat inconveniences you are bound to experience everyday as your mini-workouts. Carry your own luggage instead of having to wait for the bellhop, or take the stairs instead of the elevator every once in a while. Not only will you save money and help

Mother Nature, your stamina will also increase because of all the exercise.

7. Walk without shoes or slippers from time to time.

Walking barefoot allows you to work out the pressure points on your feet, which stimulates the blood flow in different body parts. If you are taking out the trash, forget the slippers.

8. Watch your posture.

Great posture promotes balance and stimulates your mood. When you feel that your posture begins to slump, pull your shoulders back up and stretch your neck. You may be surprised that you can stay seated longer and feel relaxed afterward. Here is a bonus – having great posture is also a shortcut to having great abs.

Week 13: Choose Your Friends

Here is the part of the challenge that can be difficult – change your circle of friends. It is quite a challenge, especially if you have shared so many happy (and not so happy) moments with them. However, there will come a time when you have to change who you hang out with if you want to change your life.

Be Around People Who Keep You Focused on Growth

When you do not wake up excited anymore, then that is a red flag. You may feel this way because your peers no longer act as your support system to keep you motivated or challenged. If you do not feel you are going to find success or at least keep yourself challenged, then you might need to change your environment.

End Codependent Cycles

You might also find that you have friends that you only hear from when they need something, and you end up in a bad situation because of them. There are also people you consider friends, but you cannot really trust. If you do not have peace of mind when they are around because you always suspect that they are up to no good, then make that proactive choice to sever your ties with them.

Yes, there will always be times when you need to burn bridges, and you do not need to feel guilty about doing that. Be honest about the way you view your relationship. You are changing relationships so you can live your life free from unnecessary baggage, and teach these people to live

33

independently as well. This may seem harsh, but it is actually a good compromise.

Get Better Role Models

You will feel motivated and excited to be successful if you are around people who also strive to improve. Surround yourself with people who are willing to help you push out of your comfort zone and help you gain additional experiences. Always hang out with a person that has made it a point to achieve success and plans to do it again

Week 14: Spend Quality Time with Your Family

If you feel like constantly distracted every day, then you might not be spending enough time with your family. Remember that having a busy schedule does not mean it is okay to stop paying attention to the people who matter. This week, make it a point to rekindle your relationship with your family by spending quality time with them. Here are some tips you can use:

1. Dine together.

If you have been relying on take out for a long time, and you have been craving something made from your own kitchen, then you have the chance to offer your family something worth bonding over. Instead of going out to dinner, you should cook for them this week. If you do not know how to cook, but you are willing to learn, you can watch online videos or use easy-to-follow recipes.

2. Schedule an activity night.

If you have a tight budget, then you do not have to treat everybody out. Organize a game night instead, or have a movie night. Put some popcorn in the microwave, and let the (affordable) fun unfold.

3. Help the kids with their homework.

It makes you a better parent if you are always there to help when your kids are having a hard time, which often happens when doing homework. Make studying a way to get to know your children better by also learning what they did in school during the day.

4. Engage in other people's hobbies.

If your spouse likes to play tennis and your kids love to play video games, then see to it that you spend time with them while they are doing the activities they love. This allows them to see that you care for their interests.

5. Read bedtime stories to your kids.

Bedtime stories are great for strengthening your bond with your children, especially the young ones. It also serves as private time for you and your child. This also gives you the opportunity to hear his or her thoughts by engaging in a private conversation

6. Take your family somewhere else.

Taking a vacation with your family allows them to feel that you are allotting time away from your other tasks and distractions, and it also brings you the perfect opportunity to catch up with them. The bonus is that you are also giving everybody some much-needed relaxation time away from the everyday life.

Week 15: Improve Your Communication Skills

Do you want to be more persuasive and appear more attractive? You do not have to spend money for that. All you need to do is to improve the way you communicate.

If you have been experiencing anxiety when talking to other people and you feel that nobody listens to you when you speak, this week will be spent learning how to catch the attention of your audience and improve your charisma. Not only can you build better relationships, you can also gain confidence. Here are some tips you can use:

1. Observe how the other person speaks.

People use several different types of speech patterns on a daily basis, and it is best to observe them. People tend to listen more to people who talk similarly to them. Pay attention to their choice of words and their body language, and mirror them. You will notice that they are more perceptive if you act the way they do.

2. Use body language.

People are actually sensitive when it comes to the way you sit and hold your body. Your body language actually tells your audience many things about you, including how interested you are in talking to them, or if you have absolutely no idea what you are talking about. Remember that what you do during the entire conversation actually tells your audience another story.

3. Do not use unnecessary fillers.

Fillers, when used too much, can be distracting, and it also tells the other person that you are unprepared or too uncomfortable to talk to them. Relax and stop fidgeting. If you are lost for words, take a deep breath, and take a minute to think about what you want to say next.

4. Be a master storyteller.

Stories are great for all occasions because they stimulate your audience's mind and set the mood. It also helps you structure your thoughts or drive home an important point. When you want to be more persuasive and connect better to an audience, include stories in the conversation.

5. Ask questions.

If you are too uncomfortable to talk or give an opinion, ask questions instead of avoiding eye contact with the other person. It also helps you fill awkward silences and clarify some points that you may have missed. If you want to build more rapport, make it a point to repeat what the other person has said from time to time.

6. Use a language fit for your audience.

Be mindful about how you use language – that is the only way to guarantee you get your point across to the other person. If you are talking to a field expert with a similar background, then feel free to use jargon you are sure the other person understands. However, if you are trying to explain a similar concept to a child, then use age-appropriate language.

7. Always listen.

If you want to be liked and understood better by other people, pay more attention to them instead of yourself. Make it a point to put the other person in the spotlight and allow him to talk more. That way, you can connect your thoughts better with his. This is also the only way to know more about the person you are talking to and to make him want to listen to you too. Validate his experiences by sharing a short anecdote of your own, and he or she will surely want to pay the favor back.

Week 16: Learn How to Troubleshoot

There are times when you have difficulty finding solutions even to the simplest problems, like on the morning of an important meeting your car does not start, and you are trying to think of what to say to your client now that you know you will be late. To avoid complicating things and to fix problems faster, the focus of this week is troubleshooting.

What You Need To Do

Troubleshooting, as you already know, is identifying the problem and applying the solution for it. However, life does not really come with manuals to help you do this. For that reason, you have to rely on logic and whatever resources are available to you. At the same time, troubleshooting does not only mean finding and applying the solution yourself – it is also finding the right kind of help.

Getting Rid of Two Culprits

Two things make you linger on a problem longer than needed: worrying and trying to handle everything at once. When you are digging too deep into the problem and trying to handle the situation yourself, knowing that you do not have the skills to fix it, then it is possible that you will sink deeper into trouble.

When faced with a problem, deal with it in a neutral manner. You achieve nothing by being too anxious or concentrating on what will happen in the future. Stop what you are doing when you know that it is not working. Think of all the possible approaches, and when one of them fails, do not beat yourself up because of it. Think of your goal, and if you know someone who can help you reach it, then ask for his or her help.

Think About Solutions, Not Problems

Scientists have found out that the human brain cannot possibly find solutions if it is too fixated on the problem. The reason is simple – the problem itself is feeding your brain negative thoughts, which prevents you from focusing on the possible solutions. This does not mean you should ignore the problem, but rather try to use solution-oriented thinking that allows you to think ahead.

Being a good troubleshooter also means not being too concerned about whose fault it is or where things went wrong.

Make Things Simple

Bad troubleshooters tend to make mountains out of molehills – like solving for the answer for 1+1 using a complex algebraic formula. There are some times when going back to the basics helps you find the most obvious answers to the most difficult problems.

Week 17: Enjoy the Simple Things

You may be fixated on achieving your biggest goals, or you may be pushing yourself beyond your limits. Doing so means you are more productive so you can get the things you want, but you also have to stop from time to time to appreciate the things you already have. This week, it is time to stop, smell the roses and enjoy the simple things.

Think About the Good Things You Already Have

When you are living the fast life, you might feel the emptiness of longing for many things. Do not become too caught up with your dreams. From time to time, enjoy what you have achieved so far.

You should think about your family and how much you value them. Your achievements would not be the same without them by your side. If you find yourself longing for that brand new sports car that one of your friends just bought, remember how proud you felt when you bought your first car. Think about the first time you took your old reliable car for a spin and how happy you have been with it since.

Keep in mind that these things are not meant to dissuade you from reaching for your dreams, but to remind yourself that you can actually create new dreams and be happy with the things you already have.

Pay Attention to Things You Normally Do Not Notice

If you have been enjoying a cup of coffee every morning before you go to work at the same diner for the past three years, did you even stop to think that you would probably not have met that jolly waiter that gives you the morning coffee every day? There are so many things you think are mundane, but without them you may not have become the person you are right now. Remember that everything happens for a reason. If you feel lost and wonder why you are the person you are right now, always remember that everything that you have seen, enjoyed, or suffered through is part of it. For that reason, always remember to appreciate the little things.

Enjoy the Life that Most People Cannot Appreciate

Always remember that even if you do not work in a big company, own a fancy car, or send your kids to an Ivy League school, you can still enjoy your life. It is quite simple – realize that everything you have is already making you happy, but it is your choice to grow and experience more things in life. You might be reaching out for more things in life, but you can also decide that you are happy right now. When you think that way, you will never have to feel pressured to achieve more. Being successful and having the edge to do things differently just became a choice you can make.

Week 18: Stop Worrying

One of the main things stopping you from living a "good life" is worry. When you worry, you allow yourself to dwell on difficulty, and you feel unnecessarily uncertain. Understand that worry causes you to lose control over your life. This week, you are going to get rid of excessive worrying and replace it with a healthier mindset.

Understand Your Situation First

There are three things you should ask yourself whenever you start to worry:

1. Is your problem real, or did you just invent it because you are thinking about the what-ifs of a situation?

2. If you are convinced that the problem is a product of mulling about a hypothetical situation, is the said situation actually possible, or even realistic?

3. If it is real, can you prepare for it or fix it, or is the problem out of your control?

When you answer these questions, you will understand that no matter what your answer is, you will come up with this conclusion: whether the problem is real or not, if you can do something or nothing about it, then there is no point in dwelling on it. Why worry about anything that you can or cannot solve? For that reason, always make it a point to challenge your anxious thoughts with the questions above. Doing so will immediately bring you back to your senses.

Stopping Worry

Worrying happens when you are not prepared or you think that you cannot handle the situation. If your problem has a solution, then brainstorm until you find it. Your list of solutions does not need to be perfect – what you need is a list that shows you can handle the situation with the resources you have. After that, commit to the best solution from the list. Once you have a plan, you will automatically stop worrying.

What should you do if you know that you cannot solve the problem? The best way to deal with it is not with worry, but by embracing your feelings. Let go and accept the fact that there is nothing you can do to solve the problem, but do not get frustrated, angry, or sad. Although these emotions are normal, you really should save them for a later time. For now, forgive yourself, accept that you are limited, and recognize that there are some things that are beyond your control.

Week 19 and 20: Love Yourself

You are now on the last leg of this challenge, and for that reason, it pays to make it extra special. You need to allot two weeks for this final leg of your challenge because it is that difficult. Your last challenge for these two weeks is to love yourself.

Why Focus On This?

By not loving yourself, you will easily fall out of commitment from all the things that you promised over the previous weeks. It is easy to neglect them because you are not placing any value on yourself.

When you love yourself, you can find the strength to continue improving. You can recover from all your failures and always have a reason to bounce back and try again.

Turn Yourself into Your Own Best Friend

How many times do you find yourself talking to yourself in a mean way? How many times do you beat yourself up for the smallest mistakes? The first thing you need to do is to stop sabotaging yourself and become your own best friend.

Accept your limitations – you cannot be on the top of everything in this world. Stop comparing yourself to others, and cherish the good qualities you already have.

For these last two weeks, make a list of all your achievements so far. It does not matter if you were not able to win an award for them. Simply write down every achievement that made you proud of yourself. Remind yourself how proud you are for being able to fall in love recklessly. Remind yourself how good it felt when you offered your seat on the bus to an old person. List all your skills and remember all the times they have saved you from trouble.

Ask Your Friends About You

You may be unaware of how important you are to other people, and for that reason, make it a point to ask some of your friends and family about what makes you important. At the same time, ask them about your good and bad qualities. If it helps, you can even record the conversation, so you have something to remind you about your good points and also the areas that need improvement.

Reward Yourself

See to it that you save some money for yourself and indulge in simple luxuries such as going for a massage, or spending time in a bubble bath with some wine. Pamper yourself. You deserve it.

Forgive Yourself

If you know you have made some bad decisions lately, talk to yourself as if you are speaking to a friend. Tell yourself that no matter what you did, you are still worthy of love and forgiveness. Also remind yourself that starting today, you know better, and you will try your best to avoid same mistakes.

The moment you forgive yourself for having limitations, you realize you are capable of doing more than you can imagine. At the end of this challenge, you will realize that you have not only gained new skills, but you have also opened yourself to having a better perspective and a healthier outlook.

Congratulations! You have completed the challenge. Now, enjoy your reward of happiness and success.

Conclusion

I hope this book was able to help you transform yourself into a person with a healthy outlook in life. At the same time, I hope this book has solved your common life problems that prevent you from living your life to the fullest. After you have completed this Life Overhaul Challenge, I hope the changes you went through made you realize that life offers a lot of promise and that you have a the choice to always achieve happiness.

The next step is to commit to the promises you have made during the past 20 weeks. See to it that you are still performing these challenges even after the 20 weeks have passed. At this point, you will realize that they have become part of your personality. Now, it is time for you to level up and create new challenges for your further improvement.

Finally, if you enjoyed this book, then I would like to ask you for a favor. Would you be kind enough to leave a review for this book on Amazon? It would be greatly appreciated!

Thank you and good luck!

www.ingramcontent.com/pod-product-compliance
Lightning Source LLC
Chambersburg PA
CBHW070503290526
45790CB00003B/1071